Rainer Maria Rilke

Fifty Poems

SELECTED AND TRANSLATED FROM THE GERMAN
BY GEOFFREY LEHMANN

NYRB/POETS

 NEW YORK REVIEW BOOKS   *New York*

THIS IS A NEW YORK REVIEW BOOK
PUBLISHED BY THE NEW YORK REVIEW OF BOOKS
207 East 32nd Street, New York, NY 10016
www.nyrb.com

For Peter Jenkins and Ralph Farrell, my German teachers at school and university, and Donald Kirby, who patiently commented on these translations. —Geoffrey Lehmann

Library of Congress Cataloging-in-Publication Data
Names: Rilke, Rainer Maria, 1875–1926 author | Lehmann, Geoffrey, 1940–
   translator | Rilke, Rainer Maria, 1875–1926 Fifty poems | Rilke, Rainer
   Maria, 1875–1926 Fifty poems. English
Title: Fifty poems / by Rainer Maria Rilke; translated by Geoffrey Lehmann.
Other titles: Fifty poems (Compilation)
Description: New York City: New York Review Books, [2025] | Series:
   New York Review Books poets | Poems in German and one in French
   with parallel English translations; critical material in English |
Identifiers: LCCN 2025016537 (print) | LCCN 2025016538 (ebook) | ISBN
   9781681379944 paperback | ISBN 9781681379951 ebook
Subjects: LCSH: Rilke, Rainer Maria, 1875–1926—Translations into English |
   LCGFT: Poetry
Classification: LCC PT2635.I65 F5413 2025 (print) | LCC PT2635.I65 (ebook) |
   DDC 831/.912—dc23/eng/20250527
LC record available at https://lccn.loc.gov/2025016537
LC ebook record available at https://lccn.loc.gov/2025

ISBN 978-1-68137-994-4
Available as an electronic book; ISBN 978-1-68137-995-1

Cover and book design by Emily Singer

The authorized representative in the EU for product safety and compliance
is eucomply OÜ, Pärnu mnt 139b-14, 11317 Tallinn, Estonia,
hello@eucompliancepartner.com, +33 757690241.

Printed in the United States of America on acid-free paper.
10 9 8 7 6 5 4 3 2 1

NEW YORK REVIEW BOOKS

POETS

RAINER MARIA RILKE (1875–1926) was born in Prague, the child of a pious, wealthy mother and a military officer who worked for the railways. For most of his adult life he led a wandering existence, with long periods spent in Germany, France, and Switzerland, as well as shorter stints in Russia, Italy, and Spain. In 1901 he married the sculptor Clara Westhoff, with whom he had a daughter. The next year he moved to Paris in order to write a monograph about Auguste Rodin, whose secretary he briefly became. After the publication of the two volumes of *New Poems* (1907, 1908) and his only novel, *The Notebooks of Malte Laurids Brigge* (1910), Rilke underwent a long crisis during which he wrote, in fits and starts, *The Duino Elegies* and, in a matter of weeks in early 1922, *Sonnets to Orpheus*. He had long been suffering from ill health when he was diagnosed with leukemia. He died soon after, at the age of fifty-one.

GEOFFREY LEHMANN is an Australian poet. His *Spring Forest* was short-listed for the T. S. Eliot Prize in 1994, and his *Poems 1957–2013* won the Australian Prime Minister's Literary Award in 2015. He co-edited with Robert Gray *Australian Poetry Since 1788*. A former chairman of the Australian Tax Research Foundation, he is a retired tax lawyer. His most recent book is *Evolutionary Geopolitics: The Road to Human Egalitarianism*.

Contents

Afterword: Impersonating Rilke in English   113

Eingang

Wer du auch seist: am Abend tritt hinaus
aus deiner Stube, drin du alles weißt;
als letztes vor der Ferne liegt dein Haus:
wer du auch seist.
Mit deinen Augen, welche müde kaum
von der verbrauchten Schwelle sich befrein,
hebst du ganz langsam einen schwarzen Baum
und stellst ihn vor den Himmel: schlank, allein.
Und hast die Welt gemacht. Und sie ist groß
und wie ein Wort, das noch im Schweigen reift.
Und wie dein Wille ihren Sinn begreift,
lassen sie deine Augen zärtlich los...

Entrance

This you must do: in the evening light
leave your small room, all you once knew,
and step into the glimmering edge of night:
this you must do.
Your house the last to go, you can be free:
lift your tired eyes and let them see
against the sky a solitary black tree,
a silent universe, immense.
Your mind watches a world grow.
You want this to be all you know.
You will it to make sense,
then your eyes tenderly let it go . . .

Aus einer Kindheit

Das Dunkeln war wie Reichtum in dem Raume,
darin der Knabe, sehr verheimlicht, saß.
Und als die Mutter eintrat wie im Traume,
erzitterte im stillen Schrank ein Glas.
Sie fühlte, wie das Zimmer sie verriet,
und küsste ihren Knaben: Bist du hier?...
Dann schauten beide bang nach dem Klavier,
denn manchen Abend hatte sie ein Lied,
darin das Kind sich seltsam tief verfing.

Es saß sehr still. Sein großes Schauen hing
an ihrer Hand, die ganz gebeugt vom Ringe,
als ob sie schwer in Schneewehn ginge,
über die weißen Tasten ging.

From a Childhood

A darkness richly permeates the room
in which the boy sits, hidden in himself.
Dreamlike, the mother enters through the gloom
and a glass tinkles on a silent shelf.
She feels the room has given her away
and bends to kiss her boy: "So you are here?" . . .
Shyly they glance at the piano she will play,
thinking of afternoons they both hold dear
and tunes that move him more than he can say.

He sits quite still. With wide-open eyes he sees
her hand, heavy with its jeweled ring, and slow
as though trudging through drifts of snow
travel across the ivory keys.

Das Abendmahl

Sie sind versammelt, staunende Verstörte,
um ihn, der wie ein Weiser sich beschließt,
und der sich fortnimmt denen er gehörte,
und der an ihnen fremd vorüberfließt.
Die alte Einsamkeit kommt über ihn,
die ihn erzog zu seinem tiefen Handeln;
nun wird er wieder durch den Ölwald wandeln,
und die ihn lieben werden vor ihm fliehn.

Er hat sie zu dem letzten Tisch entboten
und (wie ein Schuß die Vögel aus den Schoten
scheucht) scheucht er ihre Hände aus den Broten
mit seinem Wort: sie fliegen zu ihm her;
sie flattern bange durch die Tafelrunde
und suchen einen Ausgang. Aber *er*
ist überall wie eine Dämmerstunde.

The Last Supper

Astonished, bewildered they are gathered here.
He, like a wise man who makes up his mind,
breaking his ties with all those he holds dear,
is now a stranger leaving them behind.
He is visited by his old loneliness,
which showed him the great wonder he must seize,
and will again pace through the olive trees,
while those who love him will flee in distress.

He asked them, knowing he will soon be dead,
to this last meal. As birds fly up with dread,
hearing a shot, their hands shrink from the bread
and the twelve startle at his prophecy,
fluttering around the table in despair,
and scatter, seeking an escape. But *he*
like twilight arriving is everywhere.

Bangnis

Im welken Walde ist ein Vogelruf,
der sinnlos scheint in diesem welken Walde.
Und dennoch ruht der runde Vogelruf
in dieser Weile, die ihn schuf,
breit wie ein Himmel auf dem welken Walde.
Gefügig räumt sich alles in den Schrei:
Das ganze Land scheint lautlos drin zu liegen,
der große Wind scheint sich hineinzuschmiegen,
und die Minute, welche weiter will,
ist bleich und still, als ob sie Dinge wüßte,
an denen jeder sterben müßte,
aus ihm herausgestiegen.

Apprehension

In the faded wood there is a birdcall.
The birdcall seems to make no sense at all,
yet lingers in the faded wood,
a sound as round and wide as the sky.
All things fit easily inside the cry.
Mutely the landscape seems to lie in it,
the great wind seems to nestle in it,
and the impatiently ticking minute
stops and goes pale, as though it knows
things that would have us die, and rose
out of the cry.

Herbsttag

Herr: es ist Zeit. Der Sommer war sehr groß.
Leg deinen Schatten auf die Sonnenuhren,
und auf den Fluren lass die Winde los.

Befiehl den letzten Früchten voll zu sein;
gib ihnen noch zwei südlichere Tage,
dränge sie zur Vollendung hin und jage
die letzte Süße in den schweren Wein.

Wer jetzt kein Haus hat, baut sich keines mehr.
Wer jetzt allein ist, wird es lange bleiben,
wird wachen, lesen, lange Briefe schreiben
und wird in den Alleen hin und her
unruhig wandern, wenn die Blätter treiben.

Autumn Day

Lord: it is time. Let this rich summer go,
darken the sundials with your shadow,
and on bare pastures let the winds blow.

Tell the last fruits to swell on tree and vine,
grant them more southern sun—just two days' grace—
press them until they are fully ripe, and chase
the last sweetness into the heavy wine.

If you are homeless, you will find no home.
Solitary, you will remain alone,
and wake and read and write long letters,
and along empty avenues will roam,
restlessly here and there, as leaves are blown.

Abend

Der Abend wechselt langsam die Gewänder,
die ihm ein Rand von alten Bäumen hält;
du schaust: und von dir scheiden sich die Länder,
ein himmelfahrendes und eins, das fällt;

und lassen dich, zu keinem ganz gehörend,
nicht ganz so dunkel wie das Haus, das schweigt,
nicht ganz so sicher Ewiges beschwörend
wie das, was Stern wird jede Nacht und steigt—

und lassen dir (unsäglich zu entwirrn)
dein Leben bang und riesenhaft und reifend,
so daß es, bald begrenzt und bald begreifend,
abwechselnd Stein in dir wird und Gestirn.

Evening

Held by a line of ancient trees, the day
gives up its blue as it grows late;
you watch; and now your two worlds separate,
one rising, as the other falls away,

leaving you wandering in a strange half-light,
wary of that dark house that is so still,
and yet without conviction and the will
to rise up and become a star each night—

leaving you wondering as to who you are,
your timid, hopeful life that does not pause
and sometimes reaches out, sometimes withdraws,
and fluctuates in you as stone then star.

Der Auszug des verlorenen Sohnes

Nun fortzugehn von alledem Verworrnen,
das unser ist und uns doch nicht gehört,
das, wie das Wasser in den alten Bornen,
uns zitternd spiegelt und das Bild zerstört;
von allem diesen, das sich wie mit Dornen
noch einmal an uns anhängt—fortzugehn
und Das und Den,
die man schon nicht mehr sah
(so täglich waren sie und so gewöhnlich),
auf einmal anzuschauen: sanft, versöhnlich
und wie an einem Anfang und von nah;
und ahnend einzusehn, wie unpersönlich,
wie über alle hin das Leid geschah,
von dem die Kindheit voll war bis zum Rand—:
Und dann noch fortzugehen, Hand aus Hand,
als ob man ein Geheiltes neu zerrisse,
und fortzugehn: wohin? Ins Ungewisse,
weit in ein unverwandtes warmes Land,
das hinter allem Handeln wie Kulisse
gleichgültig sein wird: Garten oder Wand;
und fortzugehn: warum? Aus Drang, aus Artung,
aus Ungeduld, aus dunkler Erwartung,
aus Unverständlichkeit und Unverstand:

Dies alles auf sich nehmen und vergebens
vielleicht Gehaltnes fallen lassen, um
allein zu sterben, wissend nicht warum—

Ist das der Eingang eines neuen Lebens?

The Departure of the Prodigal Son

Now to go forth discarding all confusion,
ours, yet not anything we can possess,
the false reflections in old wells, illusion
and clinging sentiment, a wilderness
of brambles—to go forth, and to see
the This and That,
what we've stopped looking at,
(what's so familiar and so ordinary),
examine it gently without preconceptions
through fresh, forgiving eyes and understand
childhood's impersonal griefs, the overflow
of old unhappinesses and deceptions,
and still to go forth, wrenching hand from hand
and opening wounds already healed, and go—
Where? Somewhere that is strange to all you know,
a temperate and unchanging land,
a stage set that's indifferent to you, blind,
so that a wall or garden's much the same.
And go forth, why? For some quirk of the mind,
dark impatience for what you cannot name,
stupidity, trapped in a baffling game:

To do this vainly seeking more and more,
and find nothing of substance and then die
alone, not understanding why—

Or does a new life open through this door?

Der Ölbaum-Garten

Er ging hinauf unter dem grauen Laub
ganz grau und aufgelöst im Ölgelände
und legte seine Stirne voller Staub
tief in das Staubigsein der heißen Hände.

Nach allem dies. Und dieses war der Schluss.
Jetzt soll ich gehen, während ich erblinde,
und warum willst Du, dass ich sagen muss,
Du seist, wenn ich Dich selber nicht mehr finde.

Ich finde Dich nicht mehr. Nicht in mir, nein.
Nicht in den andern. Nicht in diesem Stein.
Ich finde Dich nicht mehr. Ich bin allein.

Ich bin allein mit aller Menschen Gram,
den ich durch Dich zu lindern unternahm,
der Du nicht bist. O namenlose Scham...

Später erzählte man: ein Engel kam—.

Warum ein Engel? Ach es kam die Nacht
und blätterte gleichgültig in den Bäumen.
Die Jünger rührten sich in ihren Träumen.
Warum ein Engel? Ach es kam die Nacht.

Die Nacht, die kam, war keine ungemeine;
so gehen hunderte vorbei.
Da schlafen Hunde und da liegen Steine.
Ach eine traurige, ach irgendeine,
die wartet, bis es wieder Morgen sei.

The Garden of Olives

So he walked up under the gray leaves, now
quite desperate and gray in those dry lands,
and exhausted rested his dust-streaked brow,
cupping it in his hot and dusty hands.

"After everything, this. And this, the end.
I must go now, although the way is blind,
and why do You command I must pretend
that You exist, You whom I cannot find.

"I cannot find You. No. Not in this stone.
Not where other men go. Not on my own.
No. I cannot find You. I am alone.

"Alone with all the suffering which I came
to lighten, bringing comfort in Your name,
You who do not exist. Oh nameless shame..."

Later, or so it's said, an angel came—.

But why an angel? What came was the night,
and rustled through the olives unconcerned.
The disciples slept and sometimes one turned.

It was, when it came, a quite ordinary night.
Nights like this happen everywhere.
Dogs sleep and stones lie there,
and the man praying could be anyone
waiting for the morning sun.

Denn Engel kommen nicht zu solchen Betern,
und Nächte werden nicht um solche groß.
Die Sich-Verlierenden lässt alles los,
und die sind preisgegeben von den Vätern
und ausgeschlossen aus der Mütter Schooß.

The angels do not answer such a prayer.
Such nights are hardly big enough for them.
The selfless ones will find no rest or room.
They are the sons that fathers will condemn;
and mothers will eject them from the womb.

Pietà

So seh ich, Jesus, deine Füße wieder,
die damals eines Jünglings Füße waren,
da ich sie bang entkleidete und wusch;
wie standen sie verwirrt in meinen Haaren
und wie ein weißes Wild im Dornenbusch.

So seh ich deine niegeliebten Glieder
zum erstenmal in dieser Liebesnacht.
Wir legten uns noch nie zusammen nieder,
und nun wird nur bewundert und gewacht.

Doch, siehe, deine Hände sind zerrissen—:
Geliebter, nicht von mir, von meinen Bissen.
Dein Herz steht offen und man kann hinein:
das hätte dürfen nur mein Eingang sein.

Nun bist du müde, und dein müder Mund
hat keine Lust zu meinem wehen Munde—.
O Jesus, Jesus, wann war unsre Stunde?
Wie gehn wir beide wunderlich zugrund.

Pietà

When you allowed your feet to be undressed,
timidly I washed and dried them with my hair,
just a boy's feet, confused by me and bare,
a white wild thing caught in a thorn bush then.
And now, Jesus, I see your feet again.

I see your limbs no woman has caressed,
on this our night of love, for the first time.
Not lying with you was my only crime.
I watch through the long night and cannot rest.

Your poor hands have been torn. Look at them, see,
bitten, my love, but not bitten by me.
Your heart is exposed, open to the air.
Only I should be allowed entrance there.

Your mouth does not desire mine, or my pain.
When was our hour? What did we do?
It's strange, Jesus, not easy to explain
how you were ruined and I am ruined with you.

Buddha

Als ob er horchte. Stille: eine Ferne...
Wir halten ein und hören sie nicht mehr.
Und er ist Stern. Und andre große Sterne,
die wir nicht sehen, stehen um ihn her.

O er is Alles. Wirklich, warten wir,
dass er uns sähe? Sollte er bedürfen?
Und wenn wir hier uns vor ihm niederwürfen,
er bliebe tief und träge wie ein Tier.

Denn das, was uns zu seinen Füßen reißt,
das kreist in ihm seit Millionen Jahren.
Er, der vergisst was wir erfahren
und der erfährt was uns verweist.

Rodin's Buddha statue

theme and variation on a poem by Rilke

As if he's listening. Silence: something far...
We pause, hear nothing in the immensity.
And he is Star, star after giant star,
the centre of an invisible galaxy.

He is the universe. Why do we wait
for him to see us? On a little hill,
by a gravel path, inscrutable and still...
In Rodin's garden it is growing late.

L'Ange du Méridien

Chartres

Im Sturm, der um die starke Kathedrale
wie ein Verneiner stürzt der denkt und denkt,
fühlt man sich zärtlicher mit einem Male
von deinem Lächeln zu dir hingelenkt:

lächelnder Engel, fühlende Figur,
mit einem Mund, gemacht aus hundert Munden:
gewahrst du gar nicht, wie dir unsre Stunden
abgleiten von der vollen Sonnenuhr,

auf der des Tages ganze Zahl zugleich,
gleich wirklich, steht in tiefem Gleichgewichte,
als wären alle Stunden reif und reich.

Was weißt du, Steinerner, von unserm Sein?
und hältst du mit noch seligerm Gesichte
vielleicht die Tafel in die Nacht hinein?

The Angel of the Sundial

Chartres

When the great church is battered by the storm
and the sceptical downpour of the rain,
we are surprised to find you, smiling warm
and tender, promising us hope again:

sympathetic angel, statue with a smile.
Yet with your guileless face you surely see
your sundial's thieving punctuality;
its needle's shadow stays for just a while,

its equilibrium goes only so far
across the impartial numbers, every day
our hours all rich and ripe, slipping away.

Do you know, stone one, who we really are?
Is your smile happier when there is no light
and you can show your sundial to the night?

Morgue

Da liegen sie bereit, als ob es gälte,
nachträglich eine Handlung zu erfinden,
die mit einander und mit dieser Kälte
sie zu versühnen weiß und zu verbinden;

denn das ist alles noch wie ohne Schluss.
Wasfür ein Name hätte in den Taschen
sich finden sollen? An dem Überdruss
um ihren Mund hat man herumgewaschen:

er ging nicht ab; er wurde nur ganz rein.
Die Bärte stehen, noch ein wenig härter,
doch ordentlicher im Geschmack der Wärter,

nur um die Gaffenden nicht anzuwidern.
Die Augen haben hinter ihren Lidern
sich umgewandt und schauen jetzt hinein.

Morgue

They lie there waiting, ready, as if fate
has something extra for them, a shared dream
to free them from the cold and expiate
their death, resurrecting them as a team,

since everything's suspended with no end,
coins in a pocket saved for Sunday trips,
some sweets, a letter someone did not send . . .
Boredom and scorn are etched around their lips:

and soap and scrubbing can't remove the grin.
The beards have grown, the bristles hard and black.
In fact this gives them a distinguished air—

their warders like it—visitors won't scare.
The eyes beneath their lids have all rolled back,
their only focus on the world within.

Der Panther

Im Jardin des Plantes, Paris

Sein Blick ist vom Vorübergehn der Stäbe
so müd geworden, dass er nichts mehr hält.
Ihm ist, als ob es tausend Stäbe gäbe
und hinter tausend Stäben keine Welt.

Der weiche Gang geschmeidig starker Schritte,
der sich im allerkleinsten Kreise dreht,
ist wie ein Tanz von Kraft um eine Mitte,
in der betäubt ein großer Wille steht.

Nur manchmal schiebt der Vorhang der Pupille
sich lautlos auf—. Dann geht ein Bild hinein,
geht durch der Glieder angespannte Stille—
und hört im Herzen auf zu sein.

The Panther

In the Jardin des Plantes, Paris

Backwards and forwards in the cage, his gaze
is so fatigued there's nothing it can hold.
For him there are a thousand bars, always
the same bars, and beyond the bars no world.

In a diminutive circle turning there,
the easy padding and the nonchalant stride
are a pure dance about a midpoint where
a great will is arrested, stupefied.

But sometimes the pupil's shutter flicks up
mutely—. An image entering through the eyes
travels through tense limbs, coming to a stop
in the immobile heart, and dies.

Die Gazelle

Gazella Dorcas

Verzauberte: wie kann der Einklang zweier
erwählter Worte je den Reim erreichen,
der in dir kommt und geht, wie auf ein Zeichen.
Aus deiner Stirne steigen Laub und Leier,

und alles Deine geht schon im Vergleich
durch Liebeslieder, deren Worte, weich
wie Rosenblätter, dem, der nicht mehr liest,
sich auf die Augen legen, die er schließt:

um dich zu sehen: hingetragen, als
wäre mit Sprüngen jeder Lauf geladen
und schösse nur nicht ab, solang der Hals

das Haupt ins Horchen hält: wie wenn beim Baden
im Wald die Badende sich unterbricht:
den Waldsee im gewendeten Gesicht.

The Gazelle

Gazella Dorcas

Magical one: how can the single tone
of these two words become rhymed poetry,
meanings in you we see and do not see.
Your forehead sprouts two leaves, a lyre of bone,

everything in you leads to metaphor,
rose-petal sonnets, lyrics, more and more
soft cadences, until the reader lets
his head rest on the page, sleeps and forgets:

then sees *you*: tense, about to bound away
on legs like loaded shotguns that do not
detonate, as neck and head alert, sway

and listen: so in some secluded spot
a bathing girl looks up, half in surprise:
the forest lake reflected in her eyes.

Der Schwan

Diese Mühsal, durch noch Ungetanes
schwer und wie gebunden hinzugehn,
gleicht dem ungeschaffnen Gang des Schwanes.

Und das Sterben, dieses Nichtmehrfassen
jenes Grunds, auf dem wir täglich stehn,
seinem ängstlichen Sich-Niederlassen—:

in die Wasser, die ihn sanft empfangen
und die sich, wie glücklich und vergangen,
unter ihm zurückziehn, Flut um Flut;
während er unendlich still und sicher
immer mündiger und königlicher
und gelassener zu ziehn geruht.

The Swan

Our uncompleted lives, this struggling on,
relentless, as though our limbs have all been bound,
is like the awkward waddle of the swan.

And death, this loosening, coming to a stop
and tottering upon familiar ground,
is like his anxious letting-himself-drop

into the water which accepts and flows
around him, as, imperturbable, he goes
fracturing the stillness with a widening track
of ripples following like a regal train,
and glides, composed, the king of his domain,
happy in passing and not looking back.

Die Erwachsene

Das alles stand auf ihr und war die Welt
und stand auf ihr mit allem, Angst und Gnade,
wie Bäume stehen, wachsend und gerade,
ganz Bild und bildlos wie die Bundeslade
und feierlich, wie auf ein Volk gestellt.

Und sie ertrug es; trug bis obenhin
das Fliegende, Entfliehende, Entfernte,
das Ungeheuere, noch Unerlernte
gelassen wie die Wasserträgerin
den vollen Krug. Bis mitten unterm Spiel,
verwandelnd und auf andres vorbereitend,
der erste weiße Schleier, leise gleitend,
über das aufgetane Antlitz fiel

fast undurchsichtig und sich nie mehr hebend
und irgendwie auf alle Fragen ihr
nur eine Antwort vage wiedergebend:
In dir, du Kindgewesene, in dir.

The Grown-up

All stood on her, all that has ever been
and was the world, and stood, its fears and grace,
as trees stand straight and rooted in one place,
and solemn, like the memory of a race
or Ark of God, all-seeing and not seen.

She carried it; knowledge of who they are,
the flyers, those who flee, the distant ones,
the monsters and the awkward, diffident sons,
casually like a brimming water jar
on her calm head. Then in the midst of play,
preparing, changing slowly, cell by cell,
she did not sense the first white veil that fell
across her open face, bland as the day,

almost opaque, never to lift again.
And she forgot the answers she once knew,
leaving some vagueness she could not explain:
in you, the child who you have been, in you.

Die Erblindende

Sie saß so wie die anderen beim Tee.
Mir war zuerst, als ob sie ihre Tasse
ein wenig anders als die andern fasse.
Sie lächelte einmal. Es tat fast weh.

Und als man schließlich sich erhob und sprach
und langsam und wie es der Zufall brachte
durch viele Zimmer ging (man sprach und lachte),
da sah ich sie. Sie ging den andern nach,

verhalten, so wie eine, welche gleich
wird singen müssen und vor vielen Leuten;
auf ihren hellen Augen die sich freuten
war Licht von außen wie auf einem Teich.

Sie folgte langsam und sie brauchte lang
als wäre etwas noch nicht überstiegen;
und doch: als ob, nach einem Übergang,
sie nicht mehr gehen würde, sondern fliegen.

Going Blind

She sat just like the rest of us at tea,
but then I noticed how she held her cup,
a tentativeness as she picked it up,
and a faint smile—almost painful to see.

And when we all stood up with talk and laughter,
dispersing through the rooms with idle chat,
mingling and joking about this and that,
again I saw her, trailing slowly after,

preoccupied, like someone in a daze,
who is about to sing in a strange place.
Her bright and steady eyes lit up her face,
like sunlight on a pond, an unseeing gaze.

She followed, feeling her way, hesitant, shy,
as if scaling some height she could not see,
and yet: once she crossed over, at last free,
she could stop walking and begin to fly.

Abschied

Wie hab ich das gefühlt was Abschied heißt.
Wie weiß ichs noch: ein dunkles unverwundnes
grausames Etwas, das ein Schönverbundnes
noch einmal zeigt und hinhält und zerreißt.

Wie war ich ohne Wehr, dem zuzuschauen,
das, da es mich, mich rufend, gehen ließ,
zurückblieb, so als wärens alle Frauen
und dennoch klein und weiß und nichts als dies:

Ein Winken, schon nicht mehr auf mich bezogen,
ein leise Weiterwinkendes—, schon kaum
erklärbar mehr: vielleicht ein Pflaumenbaum,
von dem ein Kuckuck hastig abgeflogen.

Parting

They call it parting and I know it well.
It arrives darkly, overwhelming you,
pretends it's holding out that fragile spell
you're losing, laughs and tears it into two.

You're facing an unbearable abyss,
when what has held you, lets go in your mind,
becoming, now it has been left behind,
all women, a white point, no more than this:

A waving, an attenuated goodbye
to something that's estranged and almost now
inexplicable: a shaking plum-tree bough
whose cuckoo has just flown into the sky.

Blaue Hortensie

So wie das letzte Grün in Farbentiegeln
sind diese Blätter, trocken, stumpf und rauh,
hinter den Blütendolden, die ein Blau
nicht auf sich tragen, nur von ferne spiegeln.

Sie spiegeln es verweint und ungenau,
als wollten sie es wiederum verlieren,
und wie in alten blauen Briefpapieren
ist Gelb in ihnen, Violett und Grau;

Verwaschnes wie an einer Kinderschürze,
Nichtmehrgetragnes, dem nichts mehr geschieht:
wie fühlt man eines kleinen Lebens Kürze.

Doch plötzlich scheint das Blau sich zu verneuen
in einer von den Dolden, und man sieht
ein rührend Blaues sich vor Grünem freuen.

Blue Hydrangea

A paintpot's last green dregs, leathery, dry,
their leaves nestle beneath the distant blue
of their pale flowerheads whose uncertain hue
is not their own, reflected from the sky.

It seems, as summer wanes, tear stained with dew,
they are resigned, ready to fade away,
and like old writing paper that was blue
they're tinged with yellow, violet, and gray;

washed out, like a child's cast off pinafore,
a useless thing that will be worn no more,
a small life, obscure in its brevity.

Yet blue seems suddenly renewed in a late
flowerhead that is opening up. We see
above the green a vivid blue vibrate.

Vor dem Sommerregen

Auf einmal ist aus allem Grün im Park
man weiß nicht was, ein Etwas, fortgenommen;
man fühlt ihn näher an die Fenster kommen
und schweigsam sein. Inständig nur und stark

ertönt aus dem Gehölz der Regenpfeifer,
man denkt an einen Hieronymus:
so sehr steigt irgend Einsamkeit und Eifer
aus dieser einen Stimme, die der Guss

erhören wird. Des Saales Wände sind
mit ihren Bildern von uns fortgetreten,
als dürften sie nicht hören was wir sagen.

Es spiegeln die verblichenen Tapeten
das ungewisse Licht von Nachmittagen,
in denen man sich fürchtete als Kind.

Before Summer Rain

The green park empties, how, you can't explain.
There is a sudden absence in the air.
It comes towards the windows, pausing there.
Out of a copse, repetitive and plain,

a golden plover pipes. A hermit's cry,
imploring fervently in the wilderness,
speaks like this bird calling in its distress
for an answering downpour from the sky.

In a long room the portraits wait for rain.
The walls are listening and they move away,
and cannot overhear the words we say.

The uncertain light on faded tapestries
brings back lost afternoons and memories.
You are afraid. You are a child again.

Letzter Abend
(Aus dem Besitze Frau Nonnas)

Und Nacht und fernes Fahren; denn der Train
des ganzen Heeres zog am Park vorüber.
Er aber hob den Blick vom Clavecin
und spielte noch und sah zu ihr hinüber

beinah wie man in einen Spiegel schaut:
so sehr erfüllt von seinen jungen Zügen
und wissend, wie sie seine Trauer trügen,
schön und verführender bei jedem Laut.

Doch plötzlich wars, als ob sich das verwische:
sie stand wie mühsam in der Fensternische
und hielt des Herzens drängendes Geklopf.

Sein Spiel gab nach. Von draußen wehte Frische.
Und seltsam fremd stand auf dem Spiegeltische
der schwarze Tschako mit dem Totenkopf.

The Last Evening
(with the permission of Frau Nonna)

A distant tramping from beyond the park—
He looks up from the clavichord. They listen:
an entire army marching in the dark.
His playing does not stop and her eyes glisten.

They exchange glances, as in a looking glass.
He knows she is fulfilled, note after note
carrying a sorrow nothing can surpass—
his fresh young features catching at her throat.

Suddenly it's pointless. Sick with unease
she stands at the bay window, weak in the knees,
and feels her heart thump. She is in a trap.

His playing stops. The air moves. A cooling breeze.
She turns and on her dressing table sees
the death's-head on the plumed black hussar's cap.

Jugend-Bildnis meines Vaters

Im Auge Traum. Die Stirn wie in Berührung
mit etwas Fernem. Um den Mund enorm
viel Jugend, ungelächelte Verführung,
und vor der vollen schmückenden Verschnürung
der schlanken adeligen Uniform
der Säbelkorb und beide Hände—, die
abwarten, ruhig, zu nichts hingedrängt.
Und nun fast nicht mehr sichtbar: als ob sie
zuerst, die Fernes greifenden, verschwänden.
Und alles andre mit sich selbst verhängt
und ausgelöscht als ob wirs nicht verständen
und tief aus seiner eignen Tiefe trüb—.

Du schnell vergehendes Daguerreotyp
in meinen langsamer vergehenden Händen.

Portrait of My Father as a Youth

The eye dreaming and the forehead remote.
The lips full of youthful vitality.
Of slender build, no smile, gentlemanly,
seductive in his aristocratic coat,
the uniform, the braid, the finery.
The sabre hilt and the two hands—unclear
and out of focus, aimlessly they stray
as if reaching for something far away,
and if they touched it, they would disappear.
Everything else shuts itself off from me,
is being erased and drawn into the past
and lightless depths that no one understands—.

Your daguerreotype fading fast
in my more slowly fading hands.

Selbstbildnis aus dem Jahre 1906

Des alten lange adligen Geschlechtes
Feststehendes im Augenbogenbau.
Im Blicke noch der Kindheit Angst und Blau
und Demut da und dort, nicht eines Knechtes
doch eines Dienenden und einer Frau.
Der Mund als Mund gemacht, groß und genau,
nicht überredend, aber ein Gerechtes
Aussagendes. Die Stirne ohne Schlechtes
und gern im Schatten stiller Niederschau.

Das, als Zusammenhang, erst nur geahnt;
noch nie im Leiden oder im Gelingen
zusammgefasst zu dauerndem Durchdringen,
doch so, als wäre mit zerstreuten Dingen
von fern ein Ernstes, Wirkliches geplant.

Self-Portrait in the Year 1906

The eyebrows from the old nobility
with their firm bone structure from bygone days.
Childhood fears lingering in the clear blue gaze,
and some occasional humility—
not abrupt—a servant's or woman's tact.
A normal mouth, the lips full and exact,
good for plain speech, but not for sophistry.
A forehead that means well and likes to be
in some quiet place alone and contemplate.

Lines join to form the countenance of a man,
a sketch, with some blank spaces left to fate
where griefs and triumphs are yet to set their seal.
It's made of bits and pieces, but it's real,
a serious work in progress with a plan.

Die Kurtisane

Venedigs Sonne wird in meinem Haar
ein Gold bereiten: aller Alchemie
erlauchten Ausgang. Meine Brauen, die
den Brücken gleichen, siehst du sie

hinführen ob der lautlosen Gefahr
der Augen, die ein heimlicher Verkehr
an die Kanäle schließt, so dass das Meer
in ihnen steigt und fällt und wechselt. Wer

mich einmal sah, beneidet meinen Hund,
weil sich auf ihm oft in zerstreuter Pause
die Hand, die nie an keiner Glut verkohlt,

die unverwundbare, geschmückt, erholt—.
Und Knaben, Hoffnungen aus altem Hause,
gehn wie an Gift an meinem Mund zugrund.

The Courtesan

Venice's sun burnishes my hair
to gold: this island city's alchemy
of light. My classic eyebrows that you see
are bridges over eyes that silently

conduct with shadows in the cool night air
a secret traffic in canals and rise
and fall like tides, with moods, pretended sighs.
If even once a stranger has set eyes

on me, he'll envy my dog. With disbelief
he'll watch my jeweled hand carelessly stray
across its pampered coat, my indifferent hand

that's never hot, pausing, distracted, bland—.
And youths, the hope of ancient houses, pay
and taste my poisonous mouth and come to grief.

Römische Fontäne

Borghese

Zwei Becken, eins das andre übersteigend
aus einem alten runden Marmorrand,
und aus dem oberen Wasser leis sich neigend
zum Wasser, welches unten wartend stand,

dem leise redenden entgegenschweigend
und heimlich, gleichsam in der hohlen Hand,
ihm Himmel hinter Grün und Dunkel zeigend
wie einen unbekannten Gegenstand;

sich selber ruhig in der schönen Schale
verbreitend ohne Heimweh, Kreis aus Kreis,
nur manchmal träumerisch und tropfenweis

sich niederlassend an den Moosbehängen
zum letzten Spiegel, der sein Becken leis
von unten lächeln macht mit Übergängen.

Roman Fountain

Borghese

Two basins, one above the other filling
an ancient pool with a curved marble rim,
the conversation of their waters spilling
from higher down to lower as they brim,

a deep stillness and loquacity blending
in the low basin like an open palm
taking droplets, ring after ring extending,
showing them bits of sky in its green calm,

like some strange object, expansive, releasing
from its carved marble shell a tranquil, cool
seepage over dark streaks of moss, unceasing,

to trickle down like drops of liquid glass
to the last mirror, the great bottom pool
which drinks them in, smiling at things that pass.

Das Karussell

Jardin du Luxembourg

Mit einem Dach und seinem Schatten dreht
sich eine kleine Weile der Bestand
von bunten Pferden, alle aus dem Land,
das lange zögert, eh es untergeht.
Zwar manche sind an Wagen angespannt,
doch alle haben Mut in ihren Mienen;
ein böser roter Löwe geht mit ihnen
und dann und wann ein weißer Elefant.

Sogar ein Hirsch ist da, ganz wie im Wald,
nur dass er einen Sattel trägt und drüber
ein kleines blaues Mädchen aufgeschnallt.

Und auf dem Löwen reitet weiß ein Junge
und hält sich mit der kleinen heißen Hand
dieweil der Löwe Zähne zeigt und Zunge.

Und dann und wann ein weißer Elefant.

Und auf den Pferden kommen sie vorüber,
auch Mädchen, helle, diesem Pferdesprunge
fast schon entwachsen; mitten in dem Schwunge
schauen sie auf, irgendwohin, herüber—

Und dann und wann ein weißer Elefant.

The Carousel

Jardin du Luxembourg

Around they go, this spinning cavalcade
of painted horses, three to every row,
storybook creatures from the afterglow
of a strange country that's about to fade.
Some hauling carriages, they show no fear,
boldly parading with their small, neat faces
as after them a fierce, red lion paces,
and a white elephant brings up the rear.

Even a stag fresh from the woods is there,
except he has a saddle and a girl
in blue, buckled up and flying through the air.

The lion displays his tongue and teeth that bite;
and a hot hand is clinging to his mane,
a small boy riding him, who's dressed in white.

And the white elephant is back again.

And as the horses go past in a whirl
shy teenage girls on wooden mounts hold tight,
awkwardly balancing, their faces bright
and glancing out at us as their skirts swirl—

And the white elephant is back again.

Und das geht hin und eilt sich, dass es endet,
und kreist und dreht sich nur und hat kein Ziel.
Ein Rot, ein Grün, ein Grau vorbeigesendet,
ein kleines kaum begonnenes Profil—.
Und manchesmal ein Lächeln, hergewendet,
ein seliges, das blendet und verschwendet
an dieses atemlose blinde Spiel...

So it goes on and hurries to its ending,
revolving to revolve it has no aim.
A red, a green, a gray are quickly blending,
a little face, that's gone before it came—.
And sometimes passing us, uncomprehending,
a happy smile that's dazzling and transcending
the breathlessness and blindness of this game . . .

Spanische Tänzerin

Wie in der Hand ein Schwefelzündholz, weiß,
eh es zur Flamme kommt, nach allen Seiten
zuckende Zungen streckt—: beginnt im Kreis
 naher Beschauer hastig, hell und heiß
ihr runder Tanz sich zuckend auszubreiten.

Und plötzlich ist er Flamme, ganz und gar.

Mit einem Blick entzündet sie ihr Haar
und dreht auf einmal mit gewagter Kunst
ihr ganzes Kleid in diese Feuersbrunst,
aus welcher sich, wie Schlangen die erschrecken,
die nackten Arme wach und klappernd strecken.

Und dann: als würde ihr das Feuer knapp,
nimmt sie es ganz zusamm und wirft es ab
sehr herrisch, mit hochmütiger Gebärde
und schaut: da liegt es rasend auf der Erde
und flammt noch immer und ergiebt sich nicht—.
Doch sieghaft, sicher und mit einem süßen
grüßenden Lächeln hebt sie ihr Gesicht
und stampft es aus mit kleinen festen Füßen.

Spanish Dancer

Just as a sulphur match, when struck, spits white
lights in your hand, spark bursting after spark,
until it flares—: her first steps in a tight
ring of spectators are abrupt, hot, bright,
then, sketching widening circles in the dark,

she suddenly ignites into her dance.

Her hair is burning from a single glance.
An artful flick and pivot on her feet
and her whole dress envelops her in heat,
and from the conflagration bare arms wake
and clacking stretch like frightened snakes and shake.

And then: as if she feels confined by it
she gathers in her fist what she has lit
and flings it incandescent on the earth
and stares down at her fire with silent mirth.
But it won't die, it splutters and still burns—.
So with a triumphant gesture and sweet
welcoming smile, gazing at us, she turns
and stamps it out with tiny, percussive feet.

Archaïscher Torso Apollos

Wir kannten nicht sein unerhörtes Haupt,
darin die Augenäpfel reiften. Aber
sein Torso glüht noch wie ein Kandelaber,
in dem sein Schauen, nur zurückgeschraubt,

sich hält und glänzt. Sonst könnte nicht der Bug
der Brust dich blenden, und im leisen Drehen
der Lenden könnte nicht ein Lächeln gehen
zu jener Mitte, die die Zeugung trug.

Sonst stünde dieser Stein entstellt und kurz
unter der Schultern durchsichtigem Sturz
und flimmerte nicht so wie Raubtierfelle;

und bräche nicht aus allen seinen Rändern
aus wie ein Stern: denn da ist keine Stelle,
die dich nicht sieht. Du mußt dein Leben ändern.

Archaic Torso of Apollo

The eyeballs ripening in the unheard-of head
do not see us, are things we cannot know,
but the hacked torso has an inner glow
where the god's gaze, subdued, lives on instead

and shines. Otherwise the broad, curving chest
would not be blinding you, nor would your eyes
follow the smile of lightly turning thighs
to their midpoint, the erased genitals' crest.

Otherwise he'd be stone, defaced, cut short,
his braced shoulders ending in empty space;
he wouldn't gleam like a carnivore's hide, taut,

cutting through all his contours like a knife,
to burst out like a star. There is no place
that does not see you. You must change your life.

Leda

Als ihn der Gott in seiner Not betrat,
erschrak er fast, den Schwan so schön zu finden,
er ließ sich ganz verwirrt in ihm verschwinden.
Schon aber trug ihn sein Betrug zur Tat,

bevor er noch des unerprobten Seins
Gefühle prüfte. Und die Aufgetane
erkannte schon den Kommenden im Schwane
und wußte schon: er bat um Eins,

das sie, verwirrt in ihrem Widerstand,
nicht mehr verbergen konnte. Er kam nieder
und halsend durch die immer schwächre Hand

ließ sich der Gott in die Geliebte los.
Dann erst empfand er glücklich sein Gefieder
und wurde wirklich Schwan in ihrem Schoß.

Leda

When he became a swan through savage need,
confused by its beauty and a strange fear
the god felt his identity disappear,
but then guile drove him to complete the deed

estranged by his new shape, each arm a wing.
The girl waited with open mouth, struck dumb,
and saw a blaze of white, the great swan come,
and knew: he wanted just one thing.

She cowered and panicked trying to withstand
this flapping god she did not want to know,
and pushed his neck back with a weakening hand.

And when confused by love they came together,
the god in ecstasy at last let go,
and was a swan in every quivering feather.

Klage um Antinous

Keiner begriff mir von euch den bithynischen Knaben
(dass ihr den Strom anfasstet und von ihm hübt...).
Ich verwöhnte ihn zwar. Und dennoch: wir haben
ihn nur mit Schwere erfüllt und für immer getrübt.

Wer vermag denn zu lieben? Wer kann es?—Noch keiner.
Und so hab ich unendliches Weh getan—.
Nun ist er am Nil der stillenden Götter einer,
und ich weiß kaum welcher und kann ihm nicht nahn.

Und ihr warfet ihn noch, Wahnsinnige, bis in die Sterne,
damit ich euch rufe und dränge: meint ihr den?
Was ist er nicht einfach ein Toter. Er wäre es gerne.
Und vielleicht wäre ihm nichts geschehn.

Lament for Antinous

None of you understood the Bythinian boy at all,
(so how the river took him, none of you could say...)
I admit I spoiled him. Yet now all of us recall
his fortitude and grace, and the real boy just fades away.

Who knows what love truly is? Or can love?—None.
I have wronged his memory for all time, I fear—.
He's a Nile god now, and I scarcely know which one,
the soothing sort of god I can never get near.

Some idiots have him looking down on us as a star.
Which one? Point to him: have it as you will.
He was a boy and is dead. That's where we are.
Without this charade he might be with us still.

Kreuzigung

Längst geübt, zum kahlen Galgenplatze
irgend ein Gesindel hinzudrängen,
ließen sich die schweren Knechte hängen,
dann und wann nur eine große Fratze

kehrend nach den abgetanen Drein.
Aber oben war das schlechte Henkern
rasch getan; und nach dem Fertigsein
ließen sich die freien Männer schlenkern.

Bis der eine (fleckig wie ein Selcher)
sagte: Hauptmann, dieser hat geschrien.
Und der Hauptmann sah vom Pferde: Welcher?
und es war ihm selbst, er hätte ihn

den Elia rufen hören. Alle
waren zuzuschauen voller Lust,
und sie hielten, dass er nicht verfalle,
gierig ihm die ganze Essiggalle
an sein schwindendes Gehust.

Denn sie hofften noch ein ganzes Spiel
und vielleicht den kommenden Elia.
Aber hinten ferne schrie Maria,
und er selber brüllte und verfiel.

Crucifixion

Long practiced in prodding useless losers
up the hill to the bare gallows-place,
they hung around, some of the big bruisers,
now and then making a leering face

at the three strung up against the sky.
Their ghastly handiwork quickly done,
relaxing now and keen for some fun,
they became bored as the hours dragged by.

One, like a butcher, blood-stained and coarse,
said, "Captain, that one just called out."
"Which one?" said the captain on his horse,
but seemed to know what it was all about.

He thought the man said: "Elijah!" All
were excited by the dying man's call,
but worried about his weakening cough—
that death was about to finish him off—
and gave him vinegar mixed with gall.

There was, they hoped, entertainment ahead.
Elijah might come and stage a play.
But Mary screamed from below, far away,
and the man bellowed and was dead.

Der Auferstandene

Er vermochte niemals bis zuletzt
ihr zu weigern oder abzuneinen,
dass sie ihrer Liebe sich berühme;
und sie sank ans Kreuz in dem Kostüme
eines Schmerzes, welches ganz besetzt
war mit ihrer Liebe größten Steinen.

Aber da sie dann, um ihn zu salben,
an das Grab kam, Tränen im Gesicht,
war er auferstanden ihrethalben,
dass er seliger ihr sage: Nicht—

Sie begriff es erst in ihrer Höhle,
wie er ihr, gestärkt durch seinen Tod,
endlich das Erleichternde der Öle
und des Rührens Vorgefühl verbot,

um aus ihr die Liebende zu formen
die sich nicht mehr zum Geliebten neigt,
weil sie, hingerissen von enormen
Stürmen, seine Stimme übersteigt.

The Risen One

He never could, right to the end,
bear to say no or turn away,
lest she might make a show of love;
and in the raiment of her grief,
bedecked with her love's greatest jewels
she knelt convulsed before the cross.

Face streaming tears beside his grave,
she'd come there, wanting to anoint him,
and found him risen for her sake,
seraphic, saying to her: "Don't—"

Later it struck her in her hovel
how strong he had become through death
as he forbade the soothing oil
and her anticipated touch.

And she must give shape to her love,
to cease her leaning on the loved one,
as now enraptured by huge storms
she reaches heights beyond his voice.

Eva

Einfach steht sie an der Kathedrale
großem Aufstieg, nah der Fensterrose,
mit dem Apfel in der Apfelpose,
schuldlos-schuldig ein für alle Male

an dem Wachsenden, das sie gebar,
seit sie aus dem Kreis der Ewigkeiten
liebend fortging, um sich durchzustreiten
durch die Erde, wie ein junges Jahr.

Ach, sie hätte gern in jenem Land
noch ein wenig weilen mögen, achtend
auf der Tiere Eintracht und Verstand.

Doch da sie den Mann entschlossen fand,
ging sie mit ihm, nach dem Tode trachtend;
und sie hatte Gott noch kaum gekannt.

Eve

Near the great rose window, sublime
and artless she does not understand
why she holds an apple in each hand,
innocently guilty through all time

for all those to whom she gave birth.
Going forth from eternity's long day,
loving she made her difficult way
across the rawly created earth.

She was reluctant to leave behind
that land of endlessly perfect weather
where the animals played and were kind.

The man was resolute. She went too
and wanted them to die together,
and God was someone she scarcely knew.

Irre im Garten

Dijon

Noch schließt die aufgegebene Kartause
sich um den Hof, als würde etwas heil.
Auch die sie jetzt bewohnen, haben Pause
und nehmen nicht am Leben draußen teil.

Was irgend kommen konnte, das verlief.
Nun gehn sie gerne mit bekannten Wegen,
und trennen sich und kommen sich entgegen,
als ob sie kreisten, willig, primitiv.

Zwar manche pflegen dort die Frühlingsbeete,
demütig, dürftig, hingekniet;
aber sie haben, wenn es keiner sieht,
eine verheimlichte, verdrehte

Gebärde für das zarte frühe Gras,
ein prüfendes, verschüchtertes Liebkosen:
denn das ist freundlich, und das Rot der Rosen
wird vielleicht drohend sein und Übermaß

und wird vielleicht schon wieder übersteigen,
was ihre Seele wiederkennt und weiß.
Dies aber lässt sich noch verschweigen:
wie gut das Gras ist und wie leis.

Madmen in the Garden

Dijon

The courtyard of the abandoned monastery
is still shut, as if something's healing there.
And those who live there now you can't call free,
but they don't know the outside world or care.

Whatever life they had, has come and gone.
They happily keep to paths they seem to know,
meeting and parting, walking to and fro
in circles, innocently shambling on.

Yet others tend the flowerbeds in the spring,
humble, in poor clothes, on their knees,
but reach out, careful that nobody sees,
for the new tender grass, a coveted thing,

with a nervous and contorted caress,
to test if it is friendly to their touch.
The red of roses is for them too much.
Perhaps it threatens them with an excess,

uncertain hopes and feelings that they dread.
They like what's known and simply understood.
And they've a secret which they leave unsaid:
how quiet the grass is, and how good.

Leichen-Wäsche

Sie hatten sich an ihn gewöhnt. Doch als
die Küchenlampe kam und unruhig brannte
im dunkeln Luftzug, war der Unbekannte
ganz unbekannt. Sie wuschen seinen Hals,

und da sie nichts von seinem Schicksal wussten,
so logen sie ein anderes zusamm,
fortwährend waschend. Eine musste husten
und ließ solang den schweren Essigschwamm

auf dem Gesicht. Da gab es eine Pause
auch für die zweite. Aus der harten Bürste
klopften die Tropfen; während seine grause
gekrampfte Hand dem ganzen Hause
beweisen wollte, dass ihn nicht mehr dürste.

Und er bewies. Sie nahmen wie betreten
eiliger jetzt mit einem kurzen Huster
die Arbeit auf, so dass an den Tapeten
ihr krummer Schatten in dem stummen Muster

sich wand und wälzte wie in einem Netze,
bis dass die Waschenden zu Ende kamen.
Die Nacht im vorhanglosen Fensterrahmen
war rücksichtslos. Und einer ohne Namen
lag bar und reinlich da und gab Gesetze.

Washing the Corpse

Both women in the draughty room had grown
used to the strange corpse brought in from the night.
Then someone fetched the flickering kitchen light,
and the unknown one really was unknown.

Washing his neck, they invented bit by bit
his story, riches mixed up with disgrace.
One of them had a nervous coughing fit
and left the vinegar sponge on his face.

The other thought she'd take a break as well.
Some droplets from her scrub brush oozed and fell.
Meanwhile his clenched claw-hand was trying to tell
the women—the whole house—his thirst was gone.
He proved his point. They looked taken aback.

Clearing their throats, they now continued on,
they washed more briskly, their movements less slack;
their bent shadows started to jerk and caper,
caught in a net, the pattern of the wallpaper...

Until they'd finished. They stood back and saw
the night in the uncurtained window frame
brutal and cold. And he who had no name
lay clean and naked, and laid down the law.

Eine Welke

Leicht, wie nach ihrem Tode
trägt sie die Handschuh, das Tuch.
Ein Duft aus ihrer Kommode
verdrängte den lieben Geruch,

an dem sie sich früher erkannte.
Jetzt fragte sie lange nicht, wer
sie sei (: eine ferne Verwandte),
und geht in Gedanken umher

und sorgt für ein ängstliches Zimmer,
das sie ordnet und schont,
weil es vielleicht noch immer
dasselbe Mädchen bewohnt.

A Faded One

With the lightness of death
she wears her shawl and gloves.
Her wardrobe deadens the breath
of the fragrances she loves,

the scents of her youth long ago.
Who she is, she no longer asks:
(some relative she used to know)
and invents for herself small tasks,

flitting anxiously in her room,
which she tidies and tends with care,
keeping it pretty for whom—
perhaps the girl who once lived there.

Der Balkon

Neapel

Von der Enge, oben, des Balkones
angeordnet wie von einem Maler
und gebunden wie zu einem Strauß
alternder Gesichter und ovaler,
klar im Abend, sehn sie idealer,
rührender und wie für immer aus.

Diese aneinander angelehnten
Schwestern, die, als ob sie sich von weit
ohne Aussicht nacheinander sehnten,
lehnen, Einsamkeit an Einsamkeit;

und der Bruder mit dem feierlichen
Schweigen, zugeschlossen, voll Geschick,
doch von einem sanften Augenblick
mit der Mutter unbemerkt verglichen;

und dazwischen, abgelebt und länglich,
längst mit keinem mehr verwandt,
einer Greisin Maske, unzugänglich,
wie im Fallen von der einen Hand

aufgehalten, während eine zweite
welkere, als ob sie weitergleite,
unten vor den Kleidern hängt zur Seite

von dem Kinder-Angesicht,
das das Letzte ist, versucht, verblichen,
von den Stäben wieder durchgestrichen
wie noch unbestimmbar, wie noch nicht.

The Balcony

Naples

High up on a narrow balcony,
a family arrangement, painterly,
as in a bouquet, packed tight,
long old faces, others young and round,
made perfect by the evening light,
they gaze out for all time, profound.

The sisters lean close, but their faces
express mutual longing and distress,
minds inhabiting distant places,
loneliness leaning on loneliness;

and the quietly ceremonious brother
is reserved, a man of destiny,
yet shows a quick kindness few may see
and an affinity with his mother;

and squeezed in, decrepit, attenuated,
a hand stretched out so she does not fall,
so ancient she seems quite unrelated,
is a crone's mask, distant from them all,

and like a claw, as if she has died,
her other hand, even more dried,
hangs detached from the dress by her side;

and last, a child's face with pale hair
peering through the iron balustrade,
broken up by bars, in light and shade,
is indefinite, as if not yet there.

Dame auf einem Balkon

Plötzlich tritt sie, in den Wind gehüllt,
licht in Lichtes, wie herausgegriffen,
während jetzt die Stube wie geschliffen
hinter ihr die Türe füllt

dunkel wie der Grund einer Kamee,
die ein Schimmern durchlässt durch die Ränder;
und du meinst der Abend war nicht, ehe
sie heraustrat, um auf das Geländer

noch ein wenig von sich fortzulegen,
noch die Hände,—um ganz leicht zu sein:
wie dem Himmel von den Häuserreihn
hingereicht, von allem zu bewegen.

Lady on a Balcony

Enveloped by wind, suddenly she
is an outline, sharply focused, bright
stepping out into the failing light
from a door you dimly see,

like a cameo chiselled from air
luminous on a background of gloom.
You had not noticed evening was there
until she stepped from her lighted room.

Hands on the railing, one in a row
of houses. No more than a glimpse, terse,
she seems quite weightless and could let go
and become the sky and universe.

Begegnung in der Kastanien-Allee

Ihm ward des Eingangs grüne Dunkelheit
kühl wie ein Seidenmantel umgegeben,
den er noch nahm und ordnete: als eben
am andern transparenten Ende, weit,

aus grüner Sonne, wie aus grünen Scheiben,
weiß eine einzelne Gestalt
aufleuchtete, um lange fern zu bleiben
und schließlich, von dem Lichterniedertreiben
bei jedem Schritte überwallt,

ein helles Wechseln auf sich herzutragen,
das scheu im Blond nach hinten lief.
Aber auf einmal war der Schatten tief,
und nahe Augen lagen aufgeschlagen

in einem neuen deutlichen Gesicht,
das wie in einem Bildnis verweilte
in dem Moment, da man sich wieder teilte:
erst war es immer, und dann war es nicht.

Encounter in the Chestnut-Allée

He felt green darkness abruptly descend
like a cool silk cloak, entering the allée.
Adjusting to the changed light, far away
he could just see at the transparent end

as though through green glass lit by a green sun,
an isolated figure, white,
that seemed a fixed point—but not quite,
as it began to move, a spot of light,
flickering, boiling, and becoming someone,

pulsating brightly, with each step it grew,
leaving a blond wake shyly in the air.
But then in sudden shadow just the two
were there, an interested stare

into the elements of a new face,
two portraits who were walking and moved on
in opposite directions and were gone:
it was forever and it left no trace.

Übung am Klavier

Der Sommer summt. Der Nachmittag macht müde;
sie atmete verwirrt ihr frisches Kleid
und legte in die triftige Etüde
die Ungeduld nach einer Wirklichkeit,

die kommen konnte: morgen, heute abend—,
die vielleicht da war, die man nur verbarg;
und vor den Fenstern, hoch und alles habend,
empfand sie plötzlich den verwöhnten Park.

Da brach sie ab; schaute hinaus, verschränkte
die Hände; wünschte sich ein langes Buch—
und schob auf einmal den Jasmingeruch
erzürnt zurück. Sie fand, dass er sie kränkte.

Piano Practice

The drone of summer. Afternoon lassitude.
A trifle confused she fluffs her crisp dress,
and playing through the peremptory etude
there's an impatience that she wants to express.

Tomorrow it may come, even tonight—,
something real. Perhaps it's just hiding there.
Suddenly the tall windows and their light
from the manicured park make her aware.

She breaks off; folds her hands, a cursory look
outside. That would calm her down, a long book.
She's fighting against an atmosphere thick
with the smell of jasmine. It makes her feel sick.

Die Sonnenuhr

Selten reicht ein Schauer feuchter Fäule
aus dem Gartenschatten, wo einander
Tropfen fallen hören und ein Wander-
vogel lautet, zu der Säule,
die in Majoran und Koriander
steht und Sommerstunden zeigt;

nur sobald die Dame (der ein Diener
nachfolgt) in dem hellen Florentiner
über ihren Rand sich neigt,
wird sie schattig und verschweigt—.

Oder wenn ein sommerlicher Regen
aufkommt aus dem wogenden Bewegen
hoher Kronen, hat sie eine Pause;
denn sie weiß die Zeit nicht auszudrücken,
die dann in den Frucht- und Blumenstücken
plötzlich glüht im weißen Gartenhause.

The Sundial

It seldom comes, a cloud of moist decay
from garden shadows where a strange birdcall
is heard, and droplets listen as they fall.
Instead, with marjoram around its base
the happy sundial tells the summer day
the hours that inch across each numeral.

But when a lady visits (a chauffeur
in dark suit following her)
and bends down to it, hat across her face,
it briefly is a shadowy, silent place—.

Or when midsummer rains buffet the trees,
the high tops billowing with unease,
the sundial, overwhelmed by showers,
pauses; and nothing tracks the hours
when fruit ripen and flowers are bright
in a white summerhouse that fills with light.

Die Flamingos

Jardin des Plantes, Paris

In Spiegelbildern wie von Fragonard
ist doch von ihrem Weiß und ihrer Röte
nicht mehr gegeben, als dir einer böte,
wenn er von seiner Freundin sagt: sie war

noch sanft von Schlaf. Denn steigen sie ins Grüne
und stehn, auf rosa Stielen leicht gedreht,
beisammen, blühend, wie in einem Beet,
verführen sie verführender als Phryne

sich selber; bis sie ihres Auges Bleiche
hinhalsend bergen in der eignen Weiche,
in welcher Schwarz und Fruchtrot sich versteckt.

Auf einmal kreischt ein Neid durch die Volière;
sie aber haben sich erstaunt gestreckt
und schreiten einzeln ins Imaginäre.

The Flamingos

Jardin des Plantes, Paris

Like girls just waking, soft, flushed with surprise,
in a tableau by Fragonard of white
and red, they pose tremulous, feather-light
reflections of each other with pale eyes.

They promenade silhouetted against green,
and stand on pink stalks, each with a poised head
as though blooming in a massed garden bed.
More seductive than courtesans they preen.

With decorously bending necks they flatter
and seduce themselves, and sink curved bills inside
their flanks where glints of black and fruit-red hide.

An envious shriek goes through the aviary.
Amazed they spread their wings and quickly scatter.
Each stalks off into the imaginary.

Persisches Heliotrop

Es könnte sein, dass dir der Rose Lob
zu laut erscheint für deine Freundin: Nimm
das schön gestickte Kraut und überstimm
mit dringend flüsterndem Heliotrop

den Bülbül, der an ihren Lieblingsplätzen
sie schreiend preist und sie nicht kennt.
Denn sieh: wie süße Worte nachts in Sätzen
beisammenstehn ganz dicht, durch nichts getrennt,
aus der Vokale wachem Violett
hindüftend durch das stille Himmelbett—:

so schließen sich vor dem gesteppten Laube
deutliche Sterne zu der seidnen Traube
und mischen, dass sie fast davon verschwimmt,
die Stille mit Vanille und mit Zimmt.

Persian Heliotrope

Perhaps you think the rose's lavish red
is too loud for your mistress. Why not take
for her this neat, embroidered plant instead?
Hearing its intimate whispers she'll forsake

the bulbul who pesters her with shrill cries,
and by her bed she'll have this shy bouquet.
Now see: the flowers are like a thousand eyes
or compact stars whose violet voices say
endearments, clinging words—a faint perfume
by the four-poster bed, filling the room—:

so flowers merge above quilted leaves, are blurred,
and the lovers' murmurs are now barely heard,
and from the massed florets' blue-purple light
cinnamon and vanilla scent the night.

Die Entführung

Oft war sie als Kind ihren Dienerinnen
entwichen, um die Nacht und den Wind
(weil sie drinnen so anders sind)
draußen zu sehn an ihrem Beginnen;

doch keine Sturmnacht hatte gewiss
den riesigen Park so in Stücke gerissen,
wie ihn jetzt ihr Gewissen zerriss,

da er sie nahm von der seidenen Leiter
und sie weitertrug, weiter, weiter...:

bis der Wagen alles war.

Und sie roch ihn, den schwarzen Wagen,
um den verhalten das Jagen stand
und die Gefahr.
Und sie fand ihn mit Kaltem ausgeschlagen;
und das Schwarze und Kalte war auch in ihr.
Sie kroch in ihren Mantelkragen
und befühlte ihr Haar, als bliebe es hier,
und hörte fremd einen Fremden sagen:
Ichbinbeidir.

The Abduction

Slipping away from nurses as a child
how she loved watching night skies fall apart,
the horizon flash, and thunderstorms start.
From indoors it wasn't nearly so wild!

But the family estate, the great leafy park
were never so shredded by a stormy night
as her conscience now, tiptoeing in the dark.

Her foot feels the silk ladder sway.
Strong arms carry her away, away, away . . . :

and the coach swallows her.

She smells it, it smells cold and black,
the coach rolling across the countryside.
The cold is inside her, a cold black fear
follows her.
She shrinks into her fur collar, dares not look back,
and soon they will be hunting far and wide.
She touches her hair—it's too dark to see—
and starts at a strange voice in her ear:
Nowyourewithme.

Rosa Hortensie

Wer nahm das Rosa an? Wer wusste auch,
dass es sich sammelte in diesen Dolden?
Wie Dinge unter Gold, die sich entgolden,
enträten sie sich sanft, wie im Gebrauch.

Dass sie für solches Rosa nichts verlangen.
Bleibt es für sie und lächelt aus der Luft?
Sind Engel da, es zärtlich zu empfangen,
wenn es vergeht, großmütig wie ein Duft?

Oder vielleicht auch geben sie es preis,
damit es nie erführe vom Verblühn.
Doch unter diesem Rosa hat ein Grün
gehorcht, das jetzt verwelkt und alles weiß.

Pink Hydrangea

Who could imagine this pink? Also who knew
how the pale buds blushed with this fugitive hue?
As gold on gilded things soon rubs away
so their red tints are fading day by day.

This wonderful pink, they let us have it free.
Is it the petals, or a trick of the air?
And as it fades, does an angel tenderly
take it and spread it like scent everywhere?

Perhaps he likes to slip away unseen
leaving them in their innocence of death.
But the flowers listen and sense autumn's breath,
as pink dies back to an all-knowing green.

Der Apfelgarten

Borgeby-Gård

Komm gleich nach dem Sonnenuntergange,
sieh das Abendgrün des Rasengrunds;
ist es nicht, als hätten wir es lange
angesammelt und erspart in uns,

um es jetzt aus Fühlen und Erinnern,
neuer Hoffnung, halbvergessnem Freun,
noch vermischt mit Dunkel aus dem Innern,
in Gedanken vor uns hinzustreun

unter Bäume wie von Dürer, die
das Gewicht von hundert Arbeitstagen
in den überfüllten Früchten tragen,
dienend, voll Geduld, versuchend, wie

das, was alle Maße übersteigt,
noch zu heben ist und hinzugeben,
wenn man willig, durch ein langes Leben
nur das Eine will und wächst und schweigt.

The Apple Orchard

Borgeby-Gård

Come with me when the sun has just set,
watch the grass in the green afterglow;
is it not something known long ago,
and stored away to be with us yet,

so now from memories left behind,
feelings and hopes we scarcely admit,
coming from a dark place in the mind,
in thought before us we scatter it

under trees etched by Dürer, which bear
the weight of a hundred working days
in a surfeit of fruit in mild air,
patient, serving, seeking to amaze

with the mass of their crop, their excess:
yet toiling to give is all they know,
and willing through a long life of stress
for this one thing, silently to grow.

Der Ball

Du Runder, der das Warme aus zwei Händen
im Fliegen, oben, fortgiebt, sorglos wie
sein Eigenes; was in den Gegenständen
nicht bleiben kann, zu unbeschwert für sie,

zu wenig Ding und doch noch Ding genug,
um nicht aus allem draußen Aufgereihten
unsichtbar plötzlich in uns einzugleiten:
das glitt in dich, du zwischen Fall und Flug

noch Unentschlossener: der, wenn er steigt,
als hätte er ihn mit hinaufgehoben,
den Wurf entführt und freilässt—, und sich neigt
und einhält und den Spielenden von oben
auf einmal eine neue Stelle zeigt,
sie ordnend wie zu einer Tanzfigur,

um dann, erwartet und erwünscht von allen,
rasch, einfach, kunstlos, ganz Natur,
dem Becher hoher Hände zuzufallen.

The Ball

You, round one, taking two hands' warmth away,
soar and let the warmth go in carefree flight,
as though your own, and too fragile to stay
in solid objects, transient and light,

a thing too small, and yet enough, poised high
away from the spectators packed in tight,
gliding above us, a dot in the sky,
and hesitating between fall and flight,

as though when rising to uplift the throw
and set it free—, until veering by chance
to a new high point punctually to show
where the arc ends, signalling you are sure,
and players reconfigure in their dance,

so then, expected, cheered by all,
plummeting, simple, artless, pure,
into two hands raised in a cup you fall.

Wilder Rosenbusch

Wie steht er da vor den Verdunkelungen
des Regenabends, jung und rein;
in seinen Ranken schenkend ausgeschwungen
und doch versunken in sein Rose-sein;

die flachen Blüten, da und dort schon offen,
jegliche ungewollt und ungepflegt:
so, von sich selbst unendlich übertroffen
und unbeschreiblich aus sich selbst erregt,

ruft er dem Wandrer, der in abendlicher
Nachdenklichkeit den Weg vorüberkommt:
Oh sieh mich stehn, sieh her, was bin ich sicher
und unbeschützt und habe was mir frommt.

Wild Rosebush

How pure it is, how vibrantly it lives,
glistening at dusk as the rain comes and goes,
How lavishly with soft new shoots it gives,
and yet it's being just itself—a rose.

Its shallow petals open here and there,
neglected, blossoming early, uninvited.
Releasing its abundance to the air,
with sap and apple scent it is excited.

And so it calls out in the fading light
to the reflective, casual passerby:
See how I stand alone. My means are slight.
My needs are few, and I am simply I.

Enfant en Rouge

Parfois elle traverse le village dans sa petite robe rouge,
toute absorbée à se contenir,
mais, malgré elle, on dirait qu'elle bouge
selon un rythme de sa vie à venir.

Elle court un peu, hésite, s'arrête,
fait demi-tour...,
et tout en rêvant secoue sa tête
contre ou pour.

Puis elle fait quelques pas d'une danse
qu'elle ébauche et oublie,
trouvant sans doute que la vie
trop vite avance.

Ce n'est pas tant qu'elle sorte
de son petit corps qui l'enferme,
mais tout ce qu'en elle elle porte
joue et germe...

C'est de cette robe qu'elle va se rappeler plus tard
dans un doux abandon;
quand toute sa vie sera pleine de hasards,
la petite robe rouge aura aura toujours raison.

Child in Red

Sometimes she wanders through the village in her red dress,
absorbed by a small world within,
but there's a jauntiness she can't repress,
the rhythm of a life yet to begin.

She runs a little, hesitates, instead
half turns upon her toes,
and dreaming, shakes her head—
which way? The Yeses or the Noes?

Then she invents the steps of an odd dance,
and forgets why she is standing there,
wondering about the why and where
of life's too swift advance.

The small capsule of her body is a toy,
something she can now enjoy,
but she is practicing for the day
when it is more than play...

And older, when she gives herself one night
to life—the rapture and distress—
she'll think of it, her small red dress,
and know that it was always, always right.

Komm du, du letzter, den ich anerkenne,
heilloser Schmerz im leiblichen Geweb:
wie ich im Geiste brannte, sieh, ich brenne
in dir; das Holz hat lange widerstrebt,
der Flamme, die du loderst, zuzustimmen,
nun aber nähr' ich dich und brenn in dir.
Mein hiesig Mildsein wird in deinem Grimmen
ein Grimm der Hölle nicht von hier.
Ganz rein, ganz planlos frei von Zukunft stieg
ich auf des Leidens wirren Scheiterhaufen,
so sicher nirgend Künftiges zu kaufen
um dieses Herz, darin der Vorrat schwieg.
Bin ich es noch, der da unkenntlich brennt?
Erinnerungen reiß ich nicht herein.
O Leben, Leben: Draußensein.
Und ich in Lohe. Niemand der mich kennt.

Come my last visitor. I know your name,
excruciating pain in every cell.
As I once burned in spirit, see how this flame
you've lit has made my body a cruel hell.
For a long time my wood resisted you.
But now my native mildness, fierce and sheer,
feeds you and burns, a fury blazing through
me, an inferno which is not from here.
Certain and free of any plan to buy
myself time, I climbed this chaotic pyre,
my heart silenced in this purposeless fire,
a person with no future, a bare I.
But is it I, burning here all alone
nameless and faceless, memory denied?
O life: to live, to be outside.
I am on fire. Someone who is unknown.

RAINER MARIA RILKE reinvented himself as a poet several times. *The Duino Elegies* and *Sonnets to Orpheus*—poems from Rilke's "late period"—have been most widely appreciated among English-speaking readers. They are often described as his masterworks.

This preference of English-speaking readers may be an accident of translation. Rilke abandoned rhyme and strict meter with *The Duino Elegies*—published in 1922. The elegies are difficult poems, but being in free form they present fewer obstacles to the translator. As a result, more than twenty translations of these elegies have been published, and although the poems' elusive meanings are difficult to tease out, translators keep trying, and readers keep reading.

W. H. Auden, who spoke German (albeit ungrammatically), wrote dismissively in his "New Year Letter" about the later Rilke, and warmly about Rilke's "thing-poems" or "Dinggedichte"—*New Poems*. The Anglo-German poet Michael Hofmann has a similar preference. Discussing Rilke's only novel, *The Notebooks of Malte Laurids Brigge* (1910), and *New Poems* of 1907 and 1908 in his Clarendon lectures, *Messing About in Boats*, Hofmann wrote: "Forget the horrid and ubiquitous *Letters to a Young Poet*, forget *Duino*, forget

The Sonnets to Orpheus. They [*New Poems*] are for me his greatest poems, and *Malte* his greatest book."

Rilke was a virtuoso with rhyme and meter, and his "thing-poems" are rhymed and in strict metrical form. In German their formal architecture has a precision that is reminiscent of a Bach partita or a Michelangelo statue. But the reliable translations into English of these poems are mostly unrhymed and not strictly metrical. They are pale shadows of Rilke's original.

There are only a few very good translations of some of Rilke's *New Poems* using rhyme and meter. One of the best known is Seamus Heaney's translation of "The Apple Orchard" which begins:

Come just after the sun has gone down, watch
This deepening of green in the evening sward...

Heaney uses a mixture of full and half rhymes and a ten-syllable line with small variations. This gives a wonderful stillness to his translation. But the voice is Heaney's rather than Rilke's. You will see from Rilke's "Der Apfelgarten," on page 102, that his lines are fully rhymed, shorter than Heaney's, and generally with nine syllables. Rilke is more highly strung. I have translated Rilke's poem sticking to his nine-syllable lines and with a quite different opening.

Why? The second line of Rilke's first stanza reads "*sieh das Abendgrün des Rasengrunds*," which translates literally as "see the evening green of the lawn." *Abendgrün* (evening green) is not standard German. It may be a neologism of Rilke's. But there is a standard German word, *Abendrot*, literally "evening red," which means "afterglow" (as of sunsets).

It is possible therefore that Rilke's *Abendgrün* refers to the green afterglow of a sunset and not to "the evening sward."

Why this should be so requires a short historical excursus. The nineteenth-century English poet Gerard Manley Hopkins wrote some letters to the leading scientific journal *Nature* about the remarkable sunsets in Europe following the Krakatoa eruption in August 1883, where there were prolonged afterglows—some of them green. The last of these letters, dated October 30, 1884, headed "The Red Light round the Sun—The Sun Blue or Green at Setting" suggested:

> A sun seen as green or blue for hours together is a phenomenon only witnessed after the late Krakatoa eruptions (barring some rare reports of like appearances after like outbreaks . . .); but a sun which turns green or blue just at setting is, I believe, an old and, we may say, ordinary one, little remarked till lately. I have a note of witnessing it, with other persons of a company, in North Wales on June 23, 1877, the sunset being very clear and bright.

Hopkins did not write a poem about the green sunsets. There were attempts by Alfred Lord Tennyson, Algernon Charles Swinburne, and Robert Seymour Bridges to use the Krakatoa sunsets as poetic material, which were failures. But Rilke, a boy living in Prague, aged seven, just turning eight late in 1883, is likely to have remembered them. Many years later he recorded this memory in "Der Apfelgarten." He seems to have seen a green afterglow at an apple orchard in Borgeby-Gård in Sweden, the setting for the poem, when he was staying with Ernest Norling and Hanna Larsson in the remains of their sixteenth-century castle.* This is apparent when you read the whole of the first stanza in my translation, which is fairly close to Rilke's original:

Come with me when the sun has just set,
watch the grass in the green afterglow;
is it not something known long ago,
and stored away to be with us yet...

"The Apple Orchard" is a miraculous poem, a metaphor for art and human achievement. It seems to recall a childhood memory, which Rilke transposes to an apple orchard in Sweden and scatters under the trees, full of apples, which, like the childhood memory, silently grow and amaze us with their excess. As well as being "mixed with darkness from inside," which I have translated as "coming from a dark place in the mind," these moments of illumination require dedication, "a hundred working days" of silent growth as the past is fulfilled in the present.

All this is said in one sentence. Proust wrote a very long novel about it. Trying to translate such a poem is a humbling experience.

I studied German for seven years at school and university. As a sixteen-year-old Australian schoolboy, or perhaps as a seventeen-year-old undergraduate, I purchased volume one of Rilke's *Sämtliche Werke* (Collected Works) in a specialist

*Morten Høi Jensen, *Difficult Death: The Life and Work of Jens Peter Jacobsen* (Yale University Press, 2017), xxv.

bookshop—these being the poems he wrote in German, 880 pages. I had fallen in love with his "thing-poems." It never occurred to me to translate them; their technical brilliance was too daunting. But I may have written a hundred or so poems under their influence. I have preserved only one of these. In 1959, when I was eighteen, it was published in *London Magazine*. In the 1960s I found my own poetic voice and Rilke ceased to be an influence.

By the time I was seventy-eight, I had written all the poems I wanted to write. My verse technique had become more secure. On a whim I translated Rilke's "The Panther." More translations followed. Each translation required a few hours of preparation, then next morning I plunged in as though I was writing a poem myself. Rhyme and meter require a concentrated flow. Over the next six years I revised the translations, trimming my extravagances to be closer to the German text.

This selection of Rilke's poems follows the order in which they appear in his *Sämtliche Werke*. The first of his poems I include, "Eingang," appears on page 371 of that volume. "Eingang" is an announcement that he is turning his back on his old self and will be a man who has no fixed abode and who rejects possessions. Up to then, with exceptions such as the marvelous "What will you do God, when I die" (which was beyond my capacity as a translator), Rilke's work is largely sentimental, rhymed tosh. But he had acquired an enormous facility with rhyme.

I have not translated any unrhymed poems in this selection. Rilke wrote some marvelous unrhymed poems. They are for others to translate. I have chosen only rhymed poems that suited my skills as a practicing poet. English, like German, is not a language where rhymes come easily. Rilke continually varied his rhyme scheme. So I felt free not to follow his often arbitrary rhyme scheme. What mattered was getting a full rhyme, so his sound world was preserved. There have been many translations of Rilke over the last hundred years or so. In a few cases I have borrowed rhymes, or a phrase, from previous translators. These include Walter Kaufmann (the rhymes for the last four lines of Rilke's last poem), Margarete Münsterberg, Helen Bridge, James McAuley, and Guntram Deichsel.

My aim with these rhymed translations is necessarily immodest: to impersonate Rilke in English. To do this, I have adjusted his expression and details where necessary to fit the meter, the available English rhymes and idiomatic flow of the English language. These betrayals of Rilke, I hope, are minor. But at all times I have tried to be true to his sound, his form and syntax (often quite convoluted), and to convey his underlying ideas. Occasionally, where Rilke's words headed that way, I have heightened an effect—sparingly, I hope—if it was implicit in the original. But the translations here are not *after* Rilke. They are intended to be *his*, not *my*, poetic voice.

German is a heavily inflected language. A German sentence tends to have significantly more syllables than the equivalent English. Preserving Rilke's sound world was as important as preserving his sense. To preserve the metrical structure of some poems, and sometimes to obtain a rhyme, I had to insert extra details into my translations. Many of the *New Poems* are like paintings from live models. To ensure a similar accuracy, I looked at photographs of different species of flamingos, Rilke's fountain in the Borghese gardens, and the torso in the Louvre that was the model for his "Archaic Torso of Apollo." I listened to recordings of a golden plover piping. I watched videos of his carousel in the Luxembourg Garden—his white elephant is now painted gray. I grew a Persian heliotrope and could detect the flowers' vanilla scent but not his cinnamon.

Rilke was born in 1875—a premature child. His mother was still mourning the loss of her first child, Ismene, who had died when a few days old the previous year. He became the only child of parents who were undistinguished members of the German-speaking ruling class in Prague.

A couple of weeks after his birth, when he was robust enough to be taken to a church, he was christened René Karl Wilhelm Johann Josef Maria. At least two of these names seem to have been chosen by his mother and were girlish: René (which rhymes with "Ismene" and is French for "born again") and Maria.

Rilke's mother combed his curls and dressed him like a girl, encouraging him to play with dolls until he was five years old. She had him kiss the wounds of Christ on a crucifix. In 1886 his parents—now separated—sent Rilke to a military academy. He was there for four traumatic years. When he was hit violently in the face, he told the classmate who hit him: "I suffer as Christ suffered quietly and without complaint, and as you hit me I pray to our dear Lord that he will forgive you." The assailant laughed, and the other boys were equally derisive when they were told about René's strange response.

His feelings about his childhood may be gathered from a

letter he wrote to Lou Andreas-Salomé in 1904, in which he described his horror of his mother, who "cannot grow old; who is empty as a garment, ghostlike and dreadful. And to think that I am her child."

In 1894 Rilke entered a commercial academy in Linz and in the following two years studied at the University of Prague without graduating. Then in 1897 he arranged for an introduction to Andreas-Salomé at a friend's apartment in Munich. She was a beautiful and charismatic woman, Rilke's elder by fifteen years, and already a published author to whom he had sent anonymous poems. She had twice rejected a proposal of marriage from Friedrich Nietzsche.

Not long after Rilke and Salomé met, they became lovers despite some initial hesitance on her part—she thought the back of his head was lacking. Salomé suggested he change the name "René" to the more masculine and Germanic "Rainer." They traveled to Russia together twice, where they met Tolstoy. Salomé spoke fluent Russian and was the daughter of a Russian general.

They continued seeing each other on their return to Berlin. They walked around the suburbs together in bare feet, Rilke affecting a peasant smock. Although René had become Rainer, he was too needy. In 1901 Salomé broke off the relationship. In 1903 after they began corresponding again, Rilke wrote to her: "I had never before, in my groping hesitancy, felt life so much..."

On April 29, 1901, two months after Salomé rejected him, Rilke married Clara Westhoff. He had met Clara at an artists' colony in Worpswede, where he may have been more attracted to her friend, the painter Paula Becker (later Modersohn-Becker, who painted an uncompleted portrait of Rilke and for whom he wrote an impassioned elegy on her early death). Salomé warned Rilke against the marriage, and Clara may already have been pregnant with their daughter, Ruth, who was born at the end of the year. In 1902 Rilke left his wife and child, and went to live in Paris. His plan was to write a monograph on the sculptor Auguste Rodin. Rilke later became Rodin's secretary.

Until his meeting with Rodin, Rilke's poetry belonged to the late nineteenth century. Much of it was decorative—clever and neat singsong. The poet Stefan George dismayed Rilke by suggesting he had begun publishing too early. As Rilke turned against his mother's Christianity, there had been a gradual deepening and darkening of tone in the years leading up to the encounter with Rodin, but his poetry was still sprinkled with mysticism. Apart from his extreme technical facility, there was little that anticipated the abrupt shift in style that was about to occur. Before Rodin, Rilke's poetry hovered in a nonphysical limbo, evoking but not describing.

When they met, the meat-eating Rodin, then in his early sixties, was stout and had a long beard, while the vegetarian Rilke was twenty-six, slender and delicate. Rodin seduced women. He kissed the stomach of a woman while she was posing for him. More often than not, Rilke was seduced. While Rilke waited for inspiration to come, Rodin told his young friend to "*travailler, toujours travailler*," work, always work. Rilke was astonished by Rodin in his studio, impetuously shaping and reshaping—by the sculptures that, even when they were complete, seemed to be in motion. During the earlier years of their friendship, Rodin set about educating his young friend, taking him on train trips to inspect the great medieval cathedrals outside Paris.

Rodin recommended to Rilke something that had been suggested to Rodin as a young sculptor: Go to the zoo and observe the animals. In November 1902 Rilke wrote what may be his most famous poem, "The Panther," with the epigraph: "*Im Jardin des Plantes, Paris.*" He must have realized there was something extraordinary about it, as he did not immediately publish it. Instead he saved it for a collection of similar poems embodying the aesthetic he absorbed from Rodin: his *Neue Gedichte* (New Poems) of 1907, which was soon followed by a companion volume, *Der Neuen Gedichte Anderer Teil* (The Other Part of the New Poems) of 1908. Together the two parts contain 173 poems.

The label of Dinggedichte, or thing-poems, seems to have been first used by the critic Kurt Oppert in 1926. There was an existing tradition of Dinggedichte in German poetry before Rilke. One of the most famous is Conrad Ferdinand Meyer's "Der römische Brunnen" (Roman Fountain) from 1882 (in my translation):

Up springs the water-jet and falling gushes
Into the round marble basin,
Which, veiling itself, overflows
Into a second basin's level;
The second gives, being too rich,
Its flood flowing into the third,
And each one takes and gives at once,
And pours and rests.

"Roman Fountain," one of Rilke's *Neue Gedichte*, may describe the same fountain in the Villa Borghese. His sonnet (on pages 58 and 59) is much more complicated than Meyer's short poem. Rilke personifies the water. The second basin responds in silence to the talking of the first basin and shows the sky to the falling water as though it is some strange object. The final basin at the bottom of the fountain responds to all this commotion by smiling that everything is transition.

Transience was Rilke's topic in a conversation with Sigmund Freud. In 1916, Freud (along with Albert Einstein, Richard Strauss, and others) contributed to a Festschrift on Goethe. Freud didn't write about Goethe. Instead he recounted a meeting in 1913 with a "young but already famous poet and a taciturn friend," when they walked through a blossoming landscape and discussed "Transience." Rilke was the young poet and the taciturn friend was Salomé.*

At a time when some English and American poets (such as T. E. Hulme, Ezra Pound, and Amy Lowell) were embracing imagism—verbal images as objects in themselves, almost bare of connotations—Rilke was also using images, but he was giving them a philosophical content. His "Roman Fountain" is an anti-imagist poem, using things to embody ideas. With no principal clause, the poem practices what it preaches—it smiles at its own ongoing transition, the ripples which spread out in never-ending circles, leaving the reader suspended. The smile in the last line is not some piece of sweet sentimentality. It is related to the archaic smile in another Rilke poem, "The Archaic Torso of Apollo."

*Sølvi Christiansen, "The psychoanalyst and the poet—a meeting between Sigmund Freud and Rainer Maria Rilke," *The Scandinavian Psychoanalytic Review* 36, no. 1 (June 27, 2013): 52–56, doi: 10.1080/01062301.2013.810009.

All of this reflects the influence of Rodin: the technical brilliance, the meticulous accuracy of observation, the continuous movement, and the fact that it expresses a philosophical viewpoint. When the second part of Rilke's *New Poems* was published in 1908, the dedication read "*A mon grand ami Auguste Rodin,*" although in May 1906 Rodin had sacked Rilke.

What makes *New Poems* "new" is how they pivot. Many nineteenth-century lyric poems end as they begin. They capture a mood. They are static. The water in Meyer's "Roman Fountain" pours and rests. That is all it does, unlike the water in Rilke's "Roman Fountain," which undergoes several transformations. Elsewhere in *New Poems* the mood changes from verse to verse, sometimes from line to line. This momentum is something Rilke learned from Rodin.

A poem's pivot is often indicated by a dash. It usually occurs about two-thirds of the way through the poem. In "The Panther" Rilke indicates this pivot in the third and final verse by a strange use of punctuation:

But sometimes the pupil's shutter flicks up
mutely—.

The dash tells the reader she has to take a deep breath. Something new is happening. In fact, in the German there is a second pivot indicated at the end of the penultimate line by a dash, as the image enters the panther's heart and ceases to exist. (The syntax of my translation did not allow me to recognize this second dash.)

None of the poems in this selection are light verse, but small verbal jokes abound—the white elephant who keeps coming back and the last line of "The Abduction." But this humor tends to be lost in unrhymed translations.

The four poems dealing with the crucifixion are among the high points of *New Poems* and rarely appear in selections of Rilke's poems in English. In "The Garden of Olives," I have indicated by quotation marks the verses which I believe are spoken by Jesus. I have translated the last three lines of this poem as:

The selfless ones will find no rest or room.
They are the sons that fathers will condemn;
and mothers will eject them from the womb.

These lines may reflect Rilke's difficult relationship with his parents, particularly his mother, and the fact that he was a premature baby.

In "Pietà" Mary Magdalene addresses the dead body of Jesus. Although the poem is not a description of a sculpture, it was probably inspired by a Rodin sculpture in which, unconventionally, Mary Magdalene, rather than Jesus's mother, Mary, watches over the body.

The third of these poems is "Crucifixion." It is easy to see why it is rarely translated. It is written in a ballad rhythm that imparts a jovial roughness to the cruel comedy described in the poem.

In the New Testament, Jesus cried out on the cross: "*Eloi, Eloi, lama sabachthani*"—"My God, my God, why hast Thou forsaken me." In this poem these words are misheard by the Roman centurion, who thinks Jesus has called on "Elia," or Elijah in English, who the centurion may not understand was an Old Testament prophet. Vinegar—cheap wine—mixed with gall is then given as a painkiller to Jesus by the Roman soldiers. In the poem they are hoping Elijah will arrive at the cross and stage a play for them. Their hopes are dashed when Mary (Jesus's mother, not Mary Magdalene) screams out to her son from far away, and he bellows and dies.

"Crucifixion" may be a metaphor for the torments Rilke suffered from other boys in the military college, where he used to compare himself to Jesus. "Crucifixion" describes an ordinary and grubby death. There is no nobility in pain, a message that Rilke repeated in the poem written just before his death.

"The Risen One" directly follows "Crucifixion" in *New Poems*, almost as an apology for the brutality of the poem that precedes it. Every line in Rilke's original is rhymed. It is written with such delicacy and precision, that I felt unable to translate it into rhymed verse. I decided on iambic tetrameter—four stressed syllables in every line.

The second verse describes how Mary Magdalene arrived at his grave to anoint him with oil, and the risen Jesus, in a state of bliss, forbade her to touch him. This verse makes the surprising comment that he had "risen for her sake." This is the first astonishing heresy in the poem—that the Son of God had risen from the dead, not to rejoin his Father but on account of Mary Magdalene. A reader familiar with Rilke will immediately relate this back to a poem in *The Book of Hours*: "Was wirst du tun Gott, wenn ich sterbe?" ("What will you do God, if I die?"), which goes on to say God only exists because of his believers.

The ___ verse describes how back in her hovel or cavern, M ___ ___ ___uzzled over Jesus's abrupt behavior. He had beco. ___ ___nce his death—the fate of many poets.

In the fourth verse, Mary Magdalene realizes Jesus wants her to cease leaning on the loved one. Enraptured by huge storms she now rises above his voice. This is a second astonishing heresy. She has risen higher than Jesus. But why higher than his voice?

The voice of the male Jesus—now risen, he sees himself as blessed—tells the emotional female Mary Magdalene not to approach. His bliss is sterile compared with her depth of feeling, her huge storm. If she can separate herself from dependence on the loved one, Ismene / Lou / Clara / Paula / Mary Magdalene can rise to a higher spiritual level than Rilke / Jesus whose epiphany exists merely in words.

This book's title, *Fifty Poems*, is slightly misleading, as there are really only forty-nine and a half Rilke translations. The half poem is one of three poems about Buddha in *New Poems*. All three of these poems seemed to me to be untranslatable into rhymed English. But rereading the first of them, I found some rhymes for the first verse and part of the second verse. I then added a few lines in my own voice, making this the one instance in this volume of what might be an adaptation, not a translation. I should add that as the book begins with some poems that predate *New Poems*, it is rounded off with three from later in Rilke's career. One of them is "Child in Red," which was written in French.

The last translation in this book is untitled. It is usually referred to by its first two words "*Komm du*"—come thou. These lines are the last entry Rilke made in his notebook. They were written in the Clinique Valmont in mid-December 1926 just a few days before he died of leukemia. The first line, "*Komm du, du letzter den ich anerkenne*," with its repeated "*du, du*," a thump, thump, reminiscent of Beethoven's

Fifth, is unforgettable, and the poem includes two other extraordinary moments. In line eight, halfway through the poem, he writes that the inferno in his body is *"nicht von hier"*—"not from here"—and he continues:

Certain and free of any plan to buy
myself time, I climbed this chaotic pyre...

In Rilke's original, which I could not replicate for metrical reasons—this pyre is "suffering's chaotic pyre"—*"des Leidens wirren Scheiterhaufen."* There is nothing noble about suffering—it is alien to us, "not from here." Rilke had been offered painkillers and refused them, not out of any exaltation of suffering but to keep his mind clear, and in this way *"Komm du,"* though written in the face of death, is life-affirming. Finally in line thirteen, there is a pivot. He asks if he is the one who is burning: Am I still I? The man who was born two months premature has had all of the identity he created for himself stripped away. He has become unknown.

—*Geoffrey Lehmann*